Really Easy G

Paul Simon

Wise Publications
London/New York/Paris/Sydney/
Copenhagen/Madrid/Tokyo

Contents

Exclusive distributors:
Music Sales Limited
8/9 Frith Street, London W1D 3JB, England.
Music Sales Pty Limited
120 Rothschild Avenue, Rosebery, NSW 2018,
Australia.

Order no. PS11550
ISBN: 0-7119-9061-1
This book ©2002 by Wise Publications

Written and arranged by Joe Bennett
Music Processed by The Pitts and Paul Ewers
Edited by Sorcha Armstrong
Book design by Chloë Alexander
Cover and book photographs courtesy of
London Features International/ Redferns
Pages 3-6 photographs by George Taylor
CD mastered by Jonas Persson

Printed in the United Kingdom by
Printwise (Haverhill) Limited, Haverhill, Suffolk.

Your Guarantee of Quality
As publishers, we strive to produce every book to
the highest commercial standards.
  The music has been freshly engraved and the
book has been carefully designed to minimise
awkward page turns and to make playing from it a
real pleasure. Particular care has been given to
specifying acid-free, neutral-sized paper made
from pulps which have not been elemental
chlorine bleached. This pulp is from farmed
sustainable forests and was produced with special
regard for the environment.
  Throughout, the printing and binding have
been planned to ensure a sturdy, attractive
publication which should give years of enjoyment.
If your copy fails to meet our high standards,
please inform us and we will gladly replace it.

Music Sales' complete catalogue describes
thousands of titles and is available in full colour
sections by subject, direct from Music Sales
Limited. Please state your areas of interest and
send a cheque/postal order for £1.50 for postage
to: Music Sales Limited, Newmarket Road,
Bury St. Edmunds, Suffolk IP33 3YB.

Got any comments?
e-mail reallyeasyguitar@musicsales.co.uk

Introduction

Welcome to Really Easy Guitar, a fantastic new way to learn the songs you love.

This book will teach you how to play 12 classic songs – and you don't even have to be able to read music!

Inside you will find lyrics and chords for each song, complete with the chord shapes you need to start playing immediately. There's a special introduction to each song, with helpful hints and playing tips. Fretboxes and guitar TAB teach you the famous riffs and patterns that everyone will recognise.

The accompanying 13-track CD features professionally recorded soundalike versions of each song – vocals have been left off so that you can sing along.

Just follow the simple four step guide to using this book and you will be ready to play along with your favourite musician!

1 Tune Your Guitar

Before you can start to play along with the backing tracks, you'll need to make sure that your guitar is in tune with the CD. Track 1 on the CD gives you notes to tune to for each string, starting with the top E string, and then working downwards.

Alternatively, tune the bottom string first and then tune all the other strings to it.

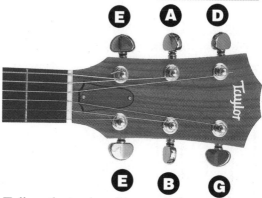

Follow the tuning diagram below and tune from the bottom string upwards.

6th to 5th string	5th to 4th string	4th to 3rd string	3rd to 2nd string	2nd to 1st string
		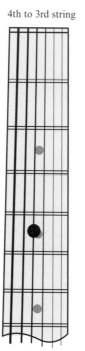		

2 Understanding fretbox diagrams

Throughout this book, fretbox diagrams are used to show chord shapes and scale patterns. Think of the box as a view of the fretboard from head on – the thickest (lowest) string is on the left and the thinnest (highest) string is on the right.

The horizontal lines correspond to the frets on your guitar; the circles indicate where you should place your fingers.

An x above the box indicates that that string should not be played; an o indicates that the string should be played open.

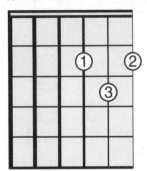

Hence, when playing this chord of D, make sure that you don't hit the bottom two strings.

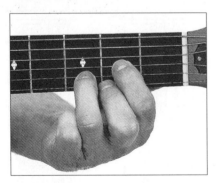

All the chords you need for each song are given at the top of the song, in the order that they appear in that song.

Am   Am/G   D9/F♯   F

Shapes that are played higher up the neck are described in the same way – the lowest fret used is indicated to the left of the box. A curved line above the box shows that a first finger barre should be used.

This barre chord of G is played at the third fret, with the first finger stretching across all six strings.

3 Understanding scale patterns

We can also use chord box diagrams to show you certain useful scale patterns on the fretboard. When a box is used to describe a scale pattern, suggested fingerings are also included.

Black circles show you the root note of the scale. If the root note of the scale is an open string, this is indicated by a double circle. Grey circles represent notes of the scale below the lowest root note.

So in this example, the root note of the scale is the open D string, with another D appearing at the third fret on the B string.

4 Understanding TAB

TAB is another easy way to learn the famous riffs and hooks in each song. The six horizontal lines represent the six strings of the guitar – the lowest line represents the lowest string (low E), while the highest line represents the highest string (high E). The number on each line tells you which fret should be played.

Although we've also included traditional music notation, you don't actually need to be able to read music to use TAB – just listen to the recording and follow the fret positions on the TAB and you'll soon be playing along. There are certain special symbols which are used:

Hammer-on

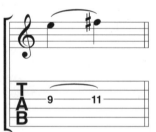

Look out for a slur connecting two numbers – when the second number is higher than the first this is called a "hammer-on". Place one finger at the lower of the two frets indicated and pick that string, then, without picking the string again, place your next finger at the higher fret. You should hear a smooth change in sound between the two notes.

Pull-off

A Pull-off is the opposite of a hammer-on, and is denoted by a slur joining two TAB numbers, where the second number is lower than the first one.

Place your fingers at the two fret positions indicated, and pick the first (higher) note, then simply lift the top finger, without picking the string again, allowing the bottom note to ring out.

Slide

A slide between two notes is denoted by a short line in the TAB. Simply play the first note, and then move your finger to the new fret position by sliding it along the fretboard, restriking the string as you arrive at the new position.

Legato slide

A legato slide is exactly the same as a normal slide, except that the second note is not picked again.

Bend

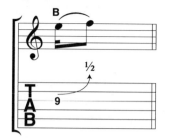

String bends are indicated as shown above – the amount that you need to bend the string is indicated near the arrow and could be q tone (a decorative bend), Q tone (the equivalent of one fret) or 1 tone (the equivalent of two frets).

Palm Muting

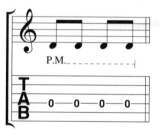

To get this percussive effect, place the side of your picking hand against the strings near the bridge as you pick.

2 Homeward Bound

From *Parsley, Sage, Rosemary & Thyme* (US) and *Sounds of Silence* (UK)

PAUL SIMON WAS 22 when he wrote 'Homeward Bound'. He was literally sitting in
a railway station (in Liverpool, 1964), having just finished playing at a folk club. And he
simply wanted to be home with his girlfriend. "The job of a folk singer in those days
was to be Bob Dylan. You had to be a poet. That's what they wanted. And I thought
that was a drag." The song was a big hit for Simon & Garfunkel, and although
Paul now describes it as 'naïve', it's still one of his best-loved tracks.

How to play it

The song sounds in the key of B♭, but on the original recording (and on our soundalike
CD version), Paul uses a capo at the 3rd fret. The intro (see tab) is played with thumb
and finger – note the 'double-stop' hammer-on in the first bar. There are several guitars
on the recording, but the main technique used is 'Travis picking' – i.e. alternating
thumb fingerstyle technique. The song sounds fine with simple strummed chords, but if
you are brave enough to attempt some simple picking patterns the results are worth it.

The song features a 'slash chord' of D/F♯. This is played by reaching the fretting
hand thumb over the top of the neck to play the second fret on the sixth string, then
fretting a normal D chord with the first, second and third fingers. Again, you don't
have to play it exactly as the original (you can just substitute a regular open D chord)
but if you can achieve this bass note without fret buzz, the fingerpicking part is
greatly improved.

For the chorus, switch from picking to strumming – listen to the CD to get the
syncopated down-up strumming pattern used by Paul. If you can quickly switch to
plectrum for this section, you'll get a more percussive rhythm sound.

Guitars

Any steel-strung acoustic should work here (Paul often favours an Ovation when
playing the song live) but do ensure that you've got decent (bronze or phosphor bronze)
strings on there. If you can manage it, a gauge of .012 or above will further enhance
the sound. There are no string bends on the original guitar part, and most of the
chords are in open positions, so there's no excuse for wimp's strings! A nylon-strung
classical guitar plays the higher-sounding arpeggios in the later verses.

▼ Intro

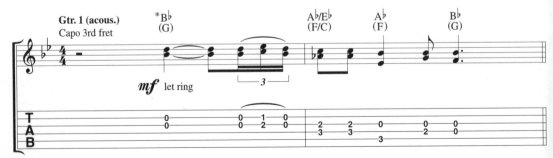

"The job of a folk singer in those days was to be Bob Dylan. You had to be a poet. That's what they wanted. And I thought that was a drag."

2 Homeward Bound

Words & Music by Paul Simon

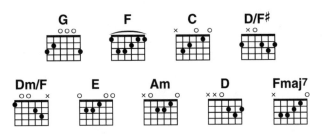

Capo third fret

Free time

Intro
| G (F) (C) G ‖

Verse 1
    G
I'm sittin' in the railway station,

    D/F♯   Dm/F   E
Got a ticket for my destination, hm-mmm.

Am
On a tour of one-night stands,

   F
My suitcase and guitar in hand,

    G
And every stop is neatly planned

    D   G
For a poet and a one man band.

Chorus 1
           C
Homeward bound,

      G
I wish I was

        C
Homeward bound,

G   Fmaj7
Home, where my thought's escaping,

G   Fmaj7
Home, where my music's playing,

G   Fmaj7
Home, where my love lies waiting

D   G
Silently for me.

Verse 2 Everyday's an endless stream

        D/F♯   **Dm/F E**

Of cigarettes and magazines, hm-mmm.

        Am

And each town looks the same to me,

      F

The movies and the factories,

      G

And every stranger's face I see

     D   **G**

Reminds me that I long to be

               C

Chorus 2   Homeward bound,

       G

I wish I was

       C

Homeward bound.

G   **Fmaj⁷**

Home, where my thought's escaping,

G   **Fmaj⁷**

Home, where my music's playing,

G   **Fmaj⁷**

Home, where my love lies waiting

D   **G**

Silently for me.

Verse 3 Tonight I'll sing my songs again,

        D/F♯   **Dm/F**   **E**

I'll play the game and pretend, hm-mmm.

        Am

But all my words come back to me

     F

In shades of mediocrity,

      G

Like emptiness in harmony,

     D   **G**

I need someone to comfort me.

Chorus 3   As Chorus 2

    D/F♯   **Dm/F**   **G (F) (C) G**

Coda   Silently for me.

(3) America

From *Bookends* (1968)

PAUL SIMON'S EARLY SONGS drew heavily on his own experiences, and 'America' is one of the best-known examples of this style of writing. It's the story of a trip he and then-girlfriend Kathy took across the country as tourists. It's also, like many of his songs of the time, a commentary on late-sixties youth in the USA. It was never released as a single, but became a concert favourite, frequently played as an encore.

How to play it

The song sounds in the key of D, but Paul starts the song on a C chord shape, so you'll need to use a capo at the second fret if you want to play along to the CD. It is just about possible to play the chords in the key of D without a capo (the main sequence works out as D, D/C♯, Bm, Bm/A), but the open chord shapes used on the original not only sound better, they're also easier to play.

Many acoustic guitarists try to play 'America' using fingerstyle techniques, but a quick listen to the CD recording will reveal that the acoustic guitar part is actually strummed throughout. The illusion of fingerstyle is created using a technique called Carter picking, where you pick a bass note with the plectrum then strum the higher notes in the gap, until it's time to pick the next bass note. The tab shows the intro, and this style of accompaniment continues with slight variations throughout the song. The full pattern should be – pluck the bass note, then strum down-up-down-up, then repeat, over a count of three – try counting "one two-and-three-and".

The song uses slash chords (i.e. chords where the bass note is different from the chord name). These are shown in the fretboxes, and because of the distinctive descending bassline in 'America', you need to play each chord exactly as shown to achieve the desired effect.

Guitar sound

There are three main guitar parts on the original recording – 12-string acoustic, 6-string acoustic, and 6-string electric guitar. The electric part uses a Leslie-type rotating speaker effect. A similar sound can be achieved on modern FX pedals by using a chorus effect and setting both the 'rate' and 'depth' control to about three-quarters of maximum.

▼ Intro

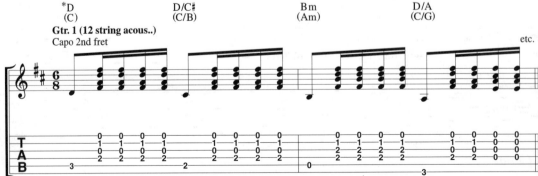

"I think it's very 1968,
kind of about a generation of kids
who have just started to travel the country."

3 America

Words & Music by Paul Simon

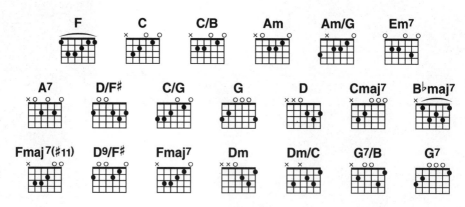

Capo second fret

Intro

N.C.   F
(Hmm-hmm-hmm-hmm-hmm hm-hm-hm,

C   C/B Am Am/G   F
Hmm-hmm-hmm-hmm-hmm hm-hm-hm.)

Verse 1

C   C/B   Am   Am/G   F
"Let us be lovers,we'll marry our fortunes together,

C   C/B   Am
I've got some real estate here in my bag".

Em⁷   A⁷   Em⁷   A⁷
So we bought a pack of cigarettes and Mrs. Wagner pies

        D/F# C/G G   C C/B Am Am/G F
And walked off to look for Ame - rica.

Verse 2

C   C/B   Am   Am/G   F
"Kathy," I said as we boarded a Greyhound in Pittsburgh,

C   C/B   Am
"Michigan seems like a dream to me now".

G
It took me four days to hitchhike from Saginaw.

D G   D   Cmaj⁷
I've gone to look for America.

Middle

B♭maj⁷
     Laughing on the bus,

        Cmaj⁷
Playing games with the faces:

B♭maj⁷   Cmaj⁷
She said the man in the gabardine suit was a spy.

F   Fmaj⁷(♯11)   C   C/B Am Am/G
I said, "Be careful his bowtie is really a camera".

Link | D9/F♯ | Fmaj⁷ ||

Verse 3

C   C/B   Am   Am/G   F
"Toss me a cigarette, I think there's one in my raincoat".

C   C/B   Am
"We smoked the last one an hour ago".

Em⁷   A⁷   Em⁷   A⁷
   So I looked at the scenery,   she read her magazine

           D/F♯ C/G G   C C/B Am Am/G F
And the moon rose over an o - pen field.

Verse 4

C   C/B Am   Am/G   F
"Kathy, I'm lost," I said, though I knew she was sleeping,

     C   Em   Am
I'm empty and aching and I don't know why.

G
Counting the cars on the New Jersey Turnpike,

        D G   D   Cmaj⁷
They've all gone to look for America,

D G   D   Cmaj⁷
All gone to look for America,

D G   D   Cmaj⁷
All gone to look for America.

Coda   ‖: C   C/B | Am Am/G | Dm Dm/C | G⁷/B G⁷ :‖ *Repeat to fade*

15

4 Mrs Robinson

From *Bookends* (1968)

MOST PEOPLE KNOW that 'Mrs Robinson' was used in the 1967 film
The Graduate, but lyrically it has very little in common with the plot of the film.
Indeed, when Paul Simon was writing it he was originally singing 'Mrs. Roosevelt'
over the chorus before agreeing with the film's producer Mike Nicholls on 'Mrs.
Robinson' as the title.

How to play it
All guitars on the recording use a capo at the 3rd fret. Consequently, the acoustic
guitar riff (see TAB) uses hammer-ons from open strings to the second fret.
The intro uses two guitars – one playing just the bass strings of the chord of E,
and the other the hammer-on riff.

The Guitar Sound
The basic (12-string) rhythm guitar sound consists of straightforward up and
down strumming. Use a plectrum, but don't hold it too firmly, letting it pivot
between the thumb and first finger of the strumming hand. The strumming motion
should come from the elbow rather than the wrist. Paul Simon is a very physical
rhythm guitarist, so you're looking for a rapid but relaxed strum over the
soundhole, skimming over the strings rather than digging into them.

Timing
The song features a time signature change into 2/4 for one bar, then back into 4/4.
This happens in every verse at the same points (in verse one, it occurs after "for
our files" and directly under "sympathetic eyes"). Rather than trying to count this
mathematically, listen to the CD recording and try to get the time change into your
brain. After a few playings it should feel quite natural, so you'll be able to strum
through it without any hiccups in the flow of the rhythm part.

▼ Intro

Mrs Robinson

Words & Music by Paul Simon

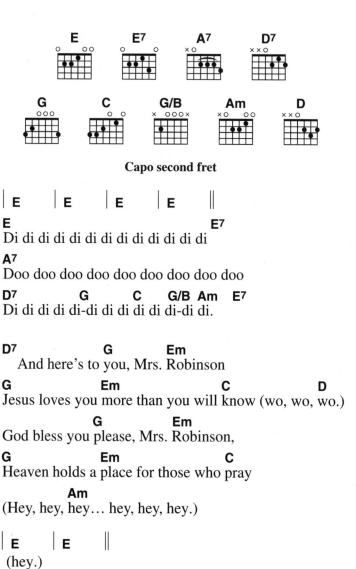

Capo second fret

Intro | E | E | E | E   ‖

E   E7
Di di di di di di di di di di di di di

A7
Doo doo doo doo doo doo doo doo doo

D7   G   C   G/B Am   E7
Di di di di di-di di di di di di-di di.

                D7   G   Em
Chorus 1   And here's to you, Mrs. Robinson
              G   Em   C   D
              Jesus loves you more than you will know (wo, wo, wo.)

                          G   Em
              God bless you please, Mrs. Robinson,
              G   Em   C
              Heaven holds a place for those who pray

                          Am
              (Hey, hey, hey… hey, hey, hey.)

              | E | E   ‖
              (hey.)

17

Mrs Robinson

Verse 1
                                                       E7
We'd like to know a little bit about you for our files,
    A7
We'd like to help you learn to help yourself.
D7   **G**   **C**   **G/B** **Am**
    Look around you, all you see are sympathetic eyes.
E7   **D7**
    Stroll around the grounds until you feel at home.

Chorus 2
                    G   **Em**
And here's to you, Mrs. Robinson,
G   **Em**   **C**   **D**
Jesus loves you more than you will know (wo, wo, wo.)
                  G   **Em**
God bless you please, Mrs. Robinson,
G   **Em**   **C**
Heaven holds a place for those who pray
        Am   **E**
(Hey, hey, hey… hey, hey, hey.)

|| E | E ||
(hey.)

Verse 2
                                                       E7
Hide it in a hiding place where no one ever goes,
A7
    Put it in your pantry with your cupcakes.
D7   **G**   **C**   **G/B**   **Am**
    It's a little secret, just the Robinsons' affair.
E   **E7**   **D7**
    Most of all, you've got to hide it from the kids.

Chorus 3
                    G   **Em**
 Coo coo ca-choo, Mrs Robinson,
G   **Em**   **C**   **D**
Jesus loves you more than you will know (wo, wo, wo.)
                  G   **Em**
God bless you please, Mrs. Robinson,
G   **Em**   **C**
Heaven holds a place for those who pray
        Am   **E**
(Hey, hey, hey… hey, hey, hey.)

|| E | E ||
(hey.)

Verse 3 Sitting on a sofa on a Sunday afternoon, **E⁷**

A⁷
 Going to the candidates' debate.

D⁷   **G**
 Laugh about it, shout about it

C   **G/B** **Am**
When you've got to choose.

E⁷   **D⁷**
 Ev'ry way you look at it, you lose.

                    G   **Em**
Chorus 4 Where have you gone, Joe DiMaggio?

 G   **Em**   **C**   **D**
A nation turns its lonely eyes to you (woo, woo, woo)

                G   **Em**
What's that you say, Mrs. Robinson?

G   **Em**   **C**
Joltin' Joe has left and gone away

            Am   **E**
(Hey, hey, hey… hey, hey, hey.)

Coda   ‖ **E**   ‖ **E**   ‖ **E**   ‖ **E**   ‖
           (hey.)   *fade*

19

5 Hazy Shade of Winter

From *Bookends* (1968)

THE PENULTIMATE SONG on the *Bookends* album, like the title track, deals with themes of old age. It was actually written several years earlier, during Paul's 'suitcase and guitar' period in the UK. The original was never released as a UK single, but the song did resurface in 1988 when The Bangles' cover version took it to number three in the charts.

How to play it
You'll notice that the CD recording sounds like two acoustic guitars are playing the intro riff at the same time. That's because of a combination of capo positioning and the 12-string's tuning. The riff is played on the three bass strings of a 12-string, with a capo at the fifth fret, which means that every note of the riff is played on a doubled-octave string pair. Don't worry, though – the notes will work just as well on a regular six-string, without the higher octave notes sounding.

The arpeggios
The verse accompaniment uses plectrum-picked arpeggios – just pick the notes of the chord one by one, fairly rapidly (in eighth notes), and let each note ring on for as long as possible before you change to the next chord. The 'chiming' quality of the chords is enhanced by that fifth fret capo position.

Picking tips
The riff and accompaniment are fairly difficult for the inexperienced player because of their speed, so here are some tips to help play it smoothly. First of all, play the whole thing with a plectrum rather than fingers, and make sure your picking hand's wrist is relaxed so you travel from string to string quickly and easily. Secondly, don't try to pick too hard. Despite the speed of the track, the picking is fairly delicate – the riff is, in fact, more difficult the harder you pick. Finally, as always with difficult lead passages, practise slowly before building up to full performance speed to ensure that each note sounds clearly without fret buzz or muted notes.

▼ Intro

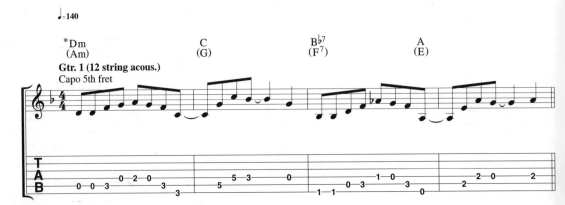

"I wouldn't normally play with a capo above the fifth fret. I don't like the sound above the fifth fret. I really don't like the sound too much above the third fret."

5 Hazy Shade of Winter

Words & Music by Paul Simon

Am   G   F   E   Am7   Cmaj7   C

Capo fifth fret

Intro | (Am) | (G) | (F) | (E) ||

Verse 1

Am   Am7 Am Am7 Am   G
Time, time, time,   see what's become of me:

        F
While I   looked around

            Cmaj7
For my possibilities

          G
I was so hard to please.

           Am   G
But look around, leaves are brown

          F   E   Am   Am7 Am
And the sky is a hazy shade of winter.

Verse 2

Am   Am7   G
Hear the Salvation Army band:

F
Down by the riverside, it's bound to be a better ride

        Cmaj7
Than what you've got planned,

          G
Carry your cup in your hand,

           Am   G
And look around, leaves are brown now

          F   E   Am
And the sky is a hazy shade of winter.

Verse 3

                G
Hang on to your hopes, my friend,

F
That's an easy thing to say, but if your hopes should pass away

Cmaj7
Simply pretend

           G
That you can build them again.

       Am   **G**
Look around, the grass is high,

              F   **E**   **Am**
The fields are ripe, it's the springtime of my life.

Bridge

  F   **C**
   Ah, seasons change with the   scenery

               G
Weaving time in a   tapestry,

                   Am
Won't you stop and remember me

G
   At any convenient time.

F
Funny how my memory skips while looking over manuscripts

     Cmaj7
Of unpublished rhyme,

           G
Drinking my vodka and lime.

       Am   **G**
I look around, leaves are brown now

        F   **E**   **Am**
And the sky is a hazy shade of winter.

Coda

         G   **F**
‖: Look around, leaves are brown,

          E   **Am**
There's a patch of snow on the ground. :‖ *Play 3 times*

6 The Boxer

From *Bridge Over Troubled Water* (1970)

BRIDGE OVER TROUBLED WATER was the last album that Simon and Garfunkel recorded together, and one of its highlights was this semi-autobiographical anthem. It also features an instrumental section written by Art Garfunkel, which is almost certainly the only example in pop music of a solo played on a lap steel guitar alongside a trumpet, recorded in a New York church!

How to play it

That rapid intro on the original was played by guitarist Fred Carter Jr, using an open tuning designed specifically to play that one bar of music. However, the rest of the song is in a version of regular tuning, although to play along with the CD version you will need to tune the whole guitar down one semitone (Eb Ab Db Gb Bb Eb).

Fingerstyle

Paul's fingerstyle chord picking (see TAB) uses alternating thumb and fingers throughout – the thumb covers the three bass strings of the guitar, and the fingers cover the remaining treble strings. An inexperienced fingerstyle player will find it almost impossible to play at this speed, so start by playing the pattern at half or even quarter speed until your fingers have 'learned' the one-bar picking pattern.

Guitar solo trivia

Yes, that bizarre, unearthly sound in the instrumental break is actually a guitar solo. According to Paul it's a lap steel guitar "with the attack off" (i.e. the start of each note is faded in), doubled on a C trumpet. The main backing track for the song was recorded in a Nashville studio, and then the horns and some of the voices were added later in New York. Despite his reputation for being picky in the studio, Paul Simon himself has rejected claims that he's a perfectionist. Still, a man hears what he wants to hear…

▼ Verse accompaniment

The Boxer

Words & Music by Paul Simon

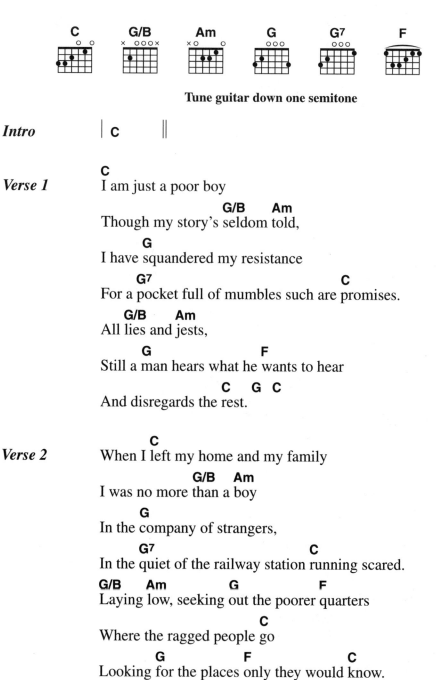

Tune guitar down one semitone

Intro | C ||

Verse 1
C
I am just a poor boy

              G/B   Am
Though my story's seldom told,

     G
I have squandered my resistance

     G7   C
For a pocket full of mumbles such are promises.

     G/B   Am
All lies and jests,

     G   F
Still a man hears what he wants to hear

                       C   G C
And disregards the rest.

Verse 2
            C
When I left my home and my family

              G/B Am
I was no more than a boy

     G
In the company of strangers,

     G7   C
In the quiet of the railway station running scared.

G/B Am   G   F
Laying low, seeking out the poorer quarters

               C
Where the ragged people go

     G   F   C
Looking for the places only they would know.

Chorus 1

    Am   **Em**
Lie la lie, lie la lie lie, lie la lie,

    Am
Lie la lie,

    G7   **C**
Lie la lie la lie la lie la la la la lie.

Verse 3

       C
Asking only workman's wages

              G/B Am
I come looking for a job

           G
But I get no offers,

      G7   **C**
Just a come-on from the whores on Seventh Avenue.

  G/B Am   **G**   **F**
I do declare, there were times when I was so lonesome

                C   **G**   **C**
I took some comfort there, la la la la la la.

Link 1

| C | C G/B Am | G | G7 | C | |
| C G/B Am | G F | F C | G F | C | ‖

Chorus 2

    Am   **Em**
Lie la lie, lie la lie lie, lie la lie,

    Am
Lie la lie,

    G7   **C**
Lie la lie la lie la lie la la la la lie.

Verse 4

       C
Then I'm laying out my winter clothes

            G/B **Am**
And wishing I was gone,

    G
Going home

           G7   **C**
Where the New York City winters aren't bleeding me,

Em   **Am**   **G**   **C**
  Bleeding me,___ going home.

Verse 5

      C
In the clearing stands a boxer

      G/B   Am
And a fighter by his trade,

     G
And he carries the reminders

     G7
Of ev'ry glove that laid him down

     C
Or cut him till he cried out

     G/B   Am
In his anger and his shame,

   G   **F**
"I am leaving, I am leaving"

          C   **G F C**
But the fighter still remains.

Chorus 3

     Am   **Em**
𝄆 Lie la lie, lie la lie lie, lie la lie

     Am
Lie la lie,

   G7   **Am**
Lie la lie la lie la lie la la la la lie. 𝄇 *Play 7 times*

Chorus 4

     Am   **Em**
Lie la lie, lie la lie lie, lie la lie

     Am
Lie la lie,

   G7   **C**
Lie la lie la lie la lie la la la la lie.

Coda | C | C G/B Am | G | G7 | C |

            | C G/B Am | G F | F C | G F | C   ‖

The Only Living Boy in New York

From *Bridge Over Troubled Water* (1970)

WHILE SIMON AND GARFUNKEL were making their final album, Art Garfunkel took a break from recording to appear in the film Catch 22. The opening line refers to him leaving for the film set; "Tom, get your plane right on time" is a reference to Tom and Jerry, the duo the two formed in the mid-1950s.

How to play it

Paul describes the song as "very much a twelve string song", and the simple chords do sound best with the instrument's characteristic lush, open chords. He uses a capo at the fourth fret, putting the song into the key of B major (although as usual our chord sheet is notated in the more guitar-friendly key of G).

The rhythm guitar part stays almost exactly the same throughout the song – it's based on a one-bar down down-up strumming pattern (the full pattern is D DU D DU DUDU DUDU). Hold the plectrum as lightly as you can without dropping it, and gently skim over the strings, making sure you make contact with each one equally. To get you started on this we've notated the 12-string part from the first two bars in the TAB below.

Chord fingering

The G chord shape might seem familiar at first, but what the TAB doesn't reveal is that Paul plays it using a different fingering. He uses his little finger to play the 3rd fret on the first (thinnest string), and the second and third fingers to play the two fretted bass notes of the chord, leaving the first finger hanging in space near the nut of the guitar. This seems a bizarre (and awkward) fingering choice until you need to change to the C chord, when the first finger is perfectly placed to make the change, and that top note rings on beautifully throughout both chords. He's in good company with this G-to-C chord shape – Bob Dylan, Bruce Springsteen, The Eagles and Tom Petty have also used it in their songs.

▼ Intro and verse strumming pattern

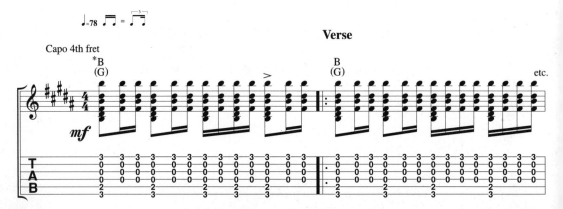

"The song was about Artie going to Mexico to make the film Catch-22. He was 'Tom' from 'Tom and Jerry'. I was wishing him well to go and make his movie."

The Only Living Boy in New York

Words & Music by Paul Simon

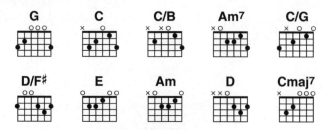

Capo fourth fret

Intro | G ‖

Verse 1

G   C
Tom, get your plane right on   time,

G   C
I know your part'll go   fine.

G   C C/B Am7 C/G
Fly down to Mexico. _____

D/F#   C
Da-n-da-da-n-da-n-da-da and here I am,

    G   C   G
The only living boy in New York.

Verse 2

G   C
I get the news I need on the weather report.

              G   C
Oh, I can gather all the news I need on the weather report.

G   C C/B Am7 C/G
Hey, I've got nothing to do to - day   but smile.

D/F#   C
    Da-n-da-da-n-da-da-n-da-da and here I am

    G   C   E
The only living boy in New York

Bridge

Am   **D**   **G**
Half of the time we're gone but we don't know where,

             C
And we don't know where.

G   **C**   **G**   **C**
(Ah _____

G   **C**   **C/B**   **Am⁷**   **C/G**   **D/F♯**
Ah _____

Cmaj⁷ G   **C**   **E**
Here I am.) _____

Am   **D**   **G**
Half of the time we're gone but we don't know where,

             C
And we don't know   where.

Verse 3

G   **C**
 Tom, get your plane right on   time.

G   **C**
I know you've been eager to fly now.

G   **C**   **C/B**   **Am⁷**   **C/G**
Hey let your honesty shine, shine, shine, now,

D/F♯
Da-n-da-da-n-da-da-n-da-da-da-da-da,

       Cmaj⁷
Like it shines on me,

     G   **C**
The only living boy in New York,

     G   **C**
The only living boy in New York.

Coda

| **G** | **G** | **G** | **C** **E** | **Am D** | **G** **C** |

G   **C**   **G**   **C**
(Ah _____

G   **C**   **C/B**   **Am⁷**   **C/G**   **D/F♯**
Ah _____

Cmaj⁷ G   **C**
Here I   am.) _____

G   **C**   **G**   **C**
(Ah _____

G   **C**   **C/B**   **Am⁷**   **C/G**   **D/F♯**
Ah _____

Cmaj⁷ G   **C**
Here I am.) _____

| **G** | |

31

8 Me and Julio Down By The Schoolyard

From *Paul Simon* (1972)

SIMON & GARFUNKEL'S FINAL ALBUM, *Bridge Over Troubled Water*, had left
Paul with a hard act to follow as a solo artist. So for his next record, entitled simply
Paul Simon, he decided on a substantial change of direction. 'Me and Julio Down By
The Schoolyard' featured Calypso-style rhythm guitar and South American influences
that were later to resurface on his 1990 album *Rhythm of the Saints*.

How to play it

The track is driven by furious up-and-down acoustic strumming in 16th notes
throughout. To get you started on this style of rhythm playing, and also hopefully to
avoid any wrist-straining accidents, let's take a look at the technique you'll need to play
in this style. Firstly, ensure that your strumming hand is as relaxed as possible,
particularly around the wrist. Next, try skimming over the strings very rapidly. Don't
dig in too deep near the soundhole, because this will slow you down. Finally, practise
'unpitched mutes' – i.e. strum across the strings, but release pressure from the fretting
hand slightly so the chord doesn't sound clearly. You can use plectrum or fingers, but
less experienced players may find the latter painful at this speed.

    The rhythmic feel of the main chord riff (see TAB) is created by strumming 16-to-
the-bar (DUDU DUDU DUDU DUDU) and using the unpitched mutes (marked as
X in the TAB) to create syncopated rhythms. Note also that one of the A chords and
the final E in each bar of the intro are played slightly earlier (i.e. the chord change
happens on an upstroke).

Cleaner chords

When you're playing at this speed, you'll find that your plectrum catches all six strings
sometimes, regardless of whether you're playing a six-string chord. This can be a
problem on the chords of A, D and B7, none of which should feature the open (bass)
E string. Paul's answer (and the one we used on our soundalike CD recording) was to
put his thumb over the top of the neck to prevent unwanted bass notes from sounding.
Do this at the same time as playing your unpitched mutes, syncopated changes and fast
down-up strumming. And, er, don't forget to keep relaxed!

▼ Intro

2 bar count in:

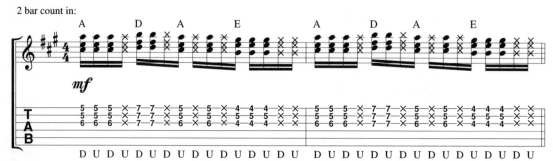

"There are no drums on that song, just percussion. We used a solid-body electric guitar miked but unamplified to get that little ringy sound you hear."

Me and Julio Down By The Schoolyard

Words & Music by Paul Simon

| A | D | E | B | G |

Intro   ‖: **A D A E** :‖   *Play 7 times*

Verse 1
           A
The mama pyjama rolled out of bed,

                 D
And she ran to the police station.

           E
When the papa found out, he began to shout,

               A
And he started the investigation.

              E   **A**
It's against the law, it was against the law,

              E   **A**
What the mama saw, it was against the law.

Verse 2
The mama looked down and spit on the ground

                 D
Every time my name gets mentioned.

E
Papa said, "Oy, if I get that boy

                             A
I'm gonna stick him in the house of detention."

Chorus 1

                    D   **A**
Well I'm on my way, I don't know where I'm goin'.

           D   **A**   **B**   **E**
I'm on my way, I'm takin' my time but I don't know where.

            D   **G**   **A**
Goodbye to Rosie, the queen of Corona.

          A   **G**   **D**   **E**   **A**   **D A E**
See you me and Julio down by the schoolyard.

          A   **G**   **D**   **E**   **A**   **D A E**
See you me and Julio down by the schoolyard.

Instr.

| D | A | D | A B E |
| D G | A | :‖ A G D E | A D A E :‖ E ‖ |

Verse 3

  A
In a couple of days they're come and take me away,

                         D
But the press let the story leak.

               E
And when the radical priest come to get me released

                  A
We was all on the cover of *Newsweek*.

Chorus 2

                   D   **A**
And I'm on my way, I don't know where I'm goin'.

           D   **A**   **B**   **E**
I'm on my way, I'm takin' my time, but I don't know where.

            D   **G**   **A**
Goodbye to Rosie, the queen of Corona.

          A   **G**   **D**   **E**   **A**   **D A E**
See you me and Julio down by the schoolyard.

          A   **G**   **D**   **E**   **A**   **D A E**
See you me and Julio down by the schoolyard.

          A   **G**   **D**   **E**   **A**   **D A E**
See you me and Julio down by the schoolyard.

Coda   ‖: **A D A E** :‖ *Repeat to fade*

From *Paul Simon* (1972)

BECAUSE PAUL SIMON is world-renowned as a fine songwriter, his guitar playing is often under-rated. Peace Like a River opens with a lively blues riff, and features swung fingerpicking, expert pre-bends and some cross-picked arpeggios that combine to make this track a lesser-known acoustic gem.

How to play it

The opening riff is not too difficult to play (see TAB), and the 2-bar sequence simply cycles round three times until the vocal enters. The notes should be allowed to 'let ring' into one another – don't play them too cleanly or you'll lose the swinging, dark blues feel of the accompaniment. Paul detunes the guitar by a whole tone (so EADGBE becomes DGCFAD). You don't have to do this to follow the chord sheet, but if you want to play along to our soundalike CD (or the original album version) you will need to take the trouble to re-tune.

The verse accompaniment

The verse accompaniment makes substantial usage of open notes – partly due to the fact that they sound better on an acoustic with heavy-gauge strings. Even if you're not following the finger pattern exactly, do try to arpeggiate the chords (i.e. pick the notes one by one) – strong down/up strumming would ruin the laid-back feel of the track.

▼ Intro riff

"I guess [Peace Like a River] was the last time that I was really sharp as an acoustic guitar player, because somewhere after that I hurt my hand and it never really healed again."

9 Peace Like a River

Words & Music by Paul Simon

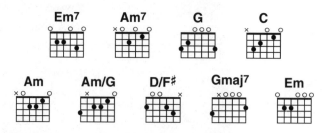

Tune guitar down a tone

Intro

Em7

Riff until vocal

Verse 1

Em7   Am7   G
Ah   peace like a river ran through the city

C   G
Long past the midnight curfew

          C   Am
We sat starry-eyed

                              Em7
Ooh, oh, we were satisfied.

Verse 2

Em7
Oh, when I remember

                            Am7   G
Misinformation followed us like a plague

C   G
Nobody knew from time to time

            C
If the plans were changed

      Am Am/G D/F#   G
Oh,   oh,   oh,   if the plans were changed.

Chorus

Am7
    You can beat us with wires

G
    You can beat us with chains

D/F♯
    You can run out your rules

                             Em7   Am7 G
But you know you can't outrun the history train

Am7
    I've seen a glorious day.

Link | Gmaj7 | Gmaj7 | D | D | Em | Em |

                                                                                      play riff

Guitar solo | Am | Am | Em | Em | Em | Em | Em7 | Em7 |

Verse 3

Em7
Oh, four in the morning

    Am7   G
I woke up from out of my dreams

C   G
Nowhere to go but back to sleep

           C   Am
But I'm reconciled

         Am Am/G D/F♯   Em7
Oh,   oh,   oh,   I'm going to be up for a while.   _Play 3 times_

Outro | Am | Am | Em | Em |

                | Em | Em | Em | Em |

                | Em | Em7 | Em | _To fade_

10 Something So Right

From *There Goes Rhymin' Simon* (1973)

IF YOU'VE JUST turned to this page from 'Peace Like a River' or 'Me and Julio…', having found the guitar parts too difficult, you may want to turn over two pages to the chord-friendly 'Kodachrome®' rather than subject your poor pinkies to any more pain. Paul's characteristic modesty about his guitar playing covers up some very tricky chord shapes in this song, but the beautiful melody and changes will make the effort well worth it.

How to play it
Paul (and session guitarist David Spinozza) originally played 'Something So Right' using a capo at the first fret, but the chord changes are equally challenging with or without it, so we've transcribed our chord sheet in the non-capo key of F major. The chords have been very slightly simplified – just enough to make them easier to play, but not so much as to lose the evocative jazz feel of the song.

For the brave…
Just to get you started, we've transcribed the intro in full in the original key (note that it requires capo at the first fret). For the even braver, the full transcription can be found in *Play Acoustic Guitar With… Paul Simon*.

▼ First four bars

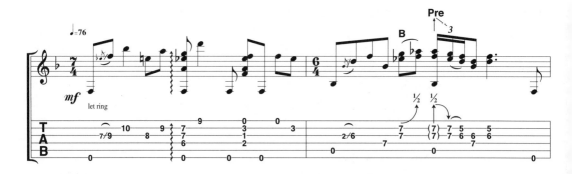

Something So Right

Words & Music by Paul Simon

[Chord diagrams: Bb/F, Fmaj7, F9, F7, Bb, Bbm7, Am7, Gm7 (fr3), Dm, C, A7aug (fr5), A7* (fr5), Dm7 (fr5), Fsus4, B7, F, C11, C/Bb, Bb7, A7, C#dim (fr3), G7, Dm, G]

Intro   N.C.

Verse 1

               Gm7 Fmaj7 F9
You've got the cool water

                     Bb   Bbm7 Am7
When the fever runs high,

Gm7   A7aug A7*   Dm7
You've got the look of lovelight in your eyes

            Fsus4 Fmaj7   F9
And I was in crazy motion

       B7   Bb   Bbm7
'Til you calmed me down,

F   Gm7
It took a little time

C11   F
But you calmed me down.

Chorus 1

        F   C/Bb
When something goes wrong

      Bb   F   F9
I'm the first to admit it,

Bb7   F
I'm the first to admit it,

Gm7   C11
And the last one to know.

F   C/Bb
When something goes right

                 F   A7
Oh it's likely to lose me, hmm,

cont.

B♭7   F9
It's apt to confuse me,

  Gm7   C♯dim Dm
It's such an unusual   sight,

  A7 B♭   F   G7
Oh, I can't, I can't get used to something so right

C11
Something so (right.)

Link 1

| B♭ F | B♭ F | Gm7 Am7 | Dm C ||
right.

Verse 2

          Gm7 Fmaj7 F9
They've got a wall in China,

            B♭ B♭m7 Am7
It's a thousand miles long,

Gm7   A7aug A7*   Dm7
To keep out the foreign - ers they made it strong.

B♭   Fsus4 Fmaj7   F9
And I've got a wall around me

       B7   B♭ B♭m7
That you can't even see.

F   Gm7
It took a little time

C11   F
To get next to me.

Chorus 2

F   C/B♭
When something goes wrong

 B♭   F F9
I'm the first to admit it,

B♭7   F
I'm the first to admit it,

Gm7   C11
And the last one to know.

F   C/B♭
When something goes right

      F A7
Well it's likely to lose me, hmm,

B♭7   F9
It's apt to confuse me, because

  Gm7 C♯dim Dm
It's such an unusual sight,

cont.

     A⁷   **B♭**   **F**   **G⁷**
Oh, I swear I can't get used to something so right
C¹¹
    Something so (right.)

Link 2   ‖ **F**   **Gm⁷** │ **Am⁷** **A⁷aug** **A⁷*** ‖
        right.

Bridge   **Dm**   **A⁷**
Some people never say the words "I love you,"
              F⁹   **B♭** **A⁷aug** **A⁷***
It's not their style to be so bold.
Dm   **A⁷**
Some people never say those words "I love you"
            Dm   **G**   **C¹¹**
But like a child they're longing to be told, hmm.

Chorus 3   **F**   **C/B♭**
When something goes wrong
B♭   **F**   **F⁹**
   I'm the first to admit it,
B♭⁷   **F**
   I'm the first to admit it
Gm⁷   **C¹¹**
   And the last one to know.
F   **C/B♭**
   When something goes right
         C¹¹   **F** **A⁷**
Well it's likely to lose me, hmm.
B♭⁷   **F⁹**
   It's apt to confuse me
        Gm⁷   **C♯dim** **Dm**
Because it's such an unusual   sight.
   A⁷   **B♭**   **Fmaj⁷** **G⁷**   **Gm⁷**
I swear, I can't, I can't get used to something so right,
C¹¹
    Something so (right.)

Coda   │ **F**   │ **Gm⁷** │ **Am⁷** │ **B♭**   │ **F** **G⁷** │ **C¹¹**   │
      right.

      ‖: **F**   │ **Gm⁷** │ **Am⁷** │ **B♭**   │ **F** **G⁷** │ **C¹¹**   :‖

                                                          Repeat to fade

11 Kodachrome®

From *There Goes Rhymin' Simon* (1973)

THE OPENING TRACK on Paul's second album after *Simon & Garfunkel* didn't make immediate friends. Not only did US radio stations dislike Paul's use of the word 'crap' in the opening line, Kodak themselves objected to the use of their trademark. Ever since then, every album sleeve and songbook (including this one) has been obliged to print that little ® after the song title.

How to play it

Luckily for many a guitarist, the song uses mainly easy open chords, largely thanks to Paul's ubiquitous capo (2nd fret). This makes the fretting hand part fairly comfortable under the fingers, leaving room for development of the unusual strumming part.

The joyous feel of the track comes from its lively tempo and unusual mix of styles – somewhere between Reggae, Calypso and Rock 'n' Roll. Take a listen to the intro and you'll hear that the D chord (which sounds as an E due to the capo) is played on the off-beat (see TAB). On the original recording (and our CD version) this is played fingerstyle, with the thumb playing the open fourth string, and the fingers plucking the three highest notes of the chord. This is quite tricky for those new to the technique, and it gets fiendishly difficult in bar 3 of the verse (after the line "…high school") because Paul plays the chords with fingers and the bass riff with his thumb – at the same time!

How to strum it

If you prefer to play the piece with a plectrum, use a downstroke to pick each bass note (usually the open fourth or fifth string) and an upstroke to catch the three thinner strings. If the bass notes prove too difficult, leave them out (they're on the backing track anyway) and just play the upstrokes. Whatever you do, don't just plough through the chords using up-down strumming throughout, or you'll spoil the effect of the intertwining rhythms created by the bass and drums.

▼ Intro picking pattern

*Symbols in parentheses represent chord names with respect to capoed gtr. (Tab 0=2nd fret)
Symbols above represent actual sounding chords

"Sometimes I sing it 'it looks better in black and white' sometimes 'it looks worse in black and white'."

11 Kodachrome®

Words & Music by Paul Simon

Chord diagrams: D, G, Em, A7, D7, B7, E, Am, C, Bm

Capo 2nd fret

Intro

| D | D | G | G | |
| Em | A7 | D | Em A7 ||

Verse 1

             D
When I think back

                           G
On all the crap I learned in high school

Em   A7   D   Em
  It's a wonder I can think at all.

A7   D
And though my lack of education

           G
Hasn't hurt me none,

Em   A7   D   D7
  I can read the writing on the wall.

Chorus 1

             G B7   E
Kodachro - - me.

                    Am   D
They give us those nice bright colours,

                G   C
They give us the greens of summers,

                  A7   D7   G B7   E
Makes you think all the world's a sunny day, oh yeah.

          Am   D   G   C
I got a Nikon camera, I love to take a photograph,

                A7   D7
So mama don't you take my Kodachrome a-(way.)

Link 1

| G | Bm | Em | A7 ||
-way.

Verse 2

                  D   D7
If you took all the girls I knew

                  G
When I was single

Em   A7   D   Em
And brought them all together for one night,

A7   D
I know they'd never match

      D7   G
My sweet imagination,

Em   A7   D
And everything looks worse in black and white.

Chorus 2

                  G B7   E
Kodachro - - me.

                      Am   D
They give us those nice bright colours,

                     G   C
They give us the greens of summers,

                      A7   D7   G B7 E
Makes you think all the world's a sunny day, oh yeah

            Am   D   G   C
I got a Nikon camera, I love to take a photograph,

                     A7   D7
So mama don't you take my Kodachrome a-(way).

Link 2

| G | Bm | Em ||
-way.

‖:   G   Bm   Em
   Mama don't take my Kodachrome away. :‖ *Play 3 times*

G   Bm
Mama don't take my Kodachrome, Mama don't take my Kodachrome,

Em
Mama don't take my Kodachrome away.

G
Double time Mama don't take my Kodachrome
feel

   Bm
Believe your boy's so far from home.

Em
Mama don't take my Kodachrome away.

G
Mama don't take my Kodachrome,

Bm   Em
Oooh-oooh, mama don't take my Kodachrome away.

‖: G | Bm | Em | Em :‖ *Repeat to fade*

47

12 Take Me to the Mardi Gras

From *There Goes Rhymin' Simon* (1973)

PAUL'S GENTLE New Orleans tribute song, originally the B-side for Kodachrome®, ended up as an A-side when it was released in the UK because the BBC refused to play music that featured brand-names. It's a beautiful track to play on guitar, not least because its fingerpicked lines are much easier to play than they sound.

How to play it

The song is based around simple chords of A, E and Bm, but the guitar part is made interesting because Paul rarely plays a complete strummed chord. Instead, he picks out double-stops (i.e. two adjacent strings together) and other 'partial chords' (i.e. any chord not using all of the available notes). For example, in bar one he plays a complicated-looking four-string shape with thumb and finger (see TAB). Look closely at these fret positions and you'll notice he's just picking out two notes from a fifth fret barre chord of 'A'. The same is true of bar three – the 9th fret double-stop actually consists of two notes taken from a 7th fret barre chord of E.

The guitar part

The original guitar part can only be played with fingers, or plectrum-and-fingers, because it uses non-adjacent strings (see bars 1-2). Keep your hand in a static position, hovering over the strings, near the soundhole, and pick fairly delicately – the song has a very laid-back feel. It's also essential to mute unwanted open strings using the fingers of either hand.

Easy version

If all of the above (and the TAB opposite) still proves too difficult, it is possible to play the song with simple strumming. Use an even up-and-down strum, holding the plectrum fairly loosely, and experiment with different rhythm patterns (DUDU UD will give a suitably 'calypso' feel). If you avoid strumming all of the strings, all of the time, you'll go some way toward recreating the feel of the partial chords used on the original recording.

▼ Chorus

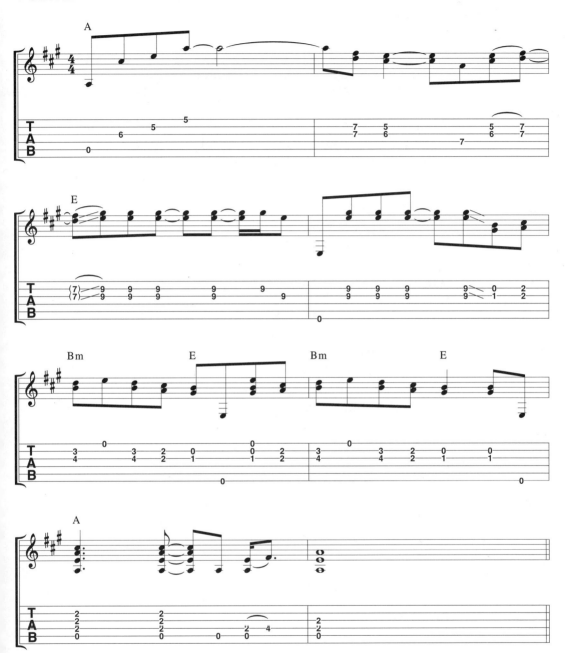

12 Take Me to the Mardi Gras

Words & Music by Paul Simon

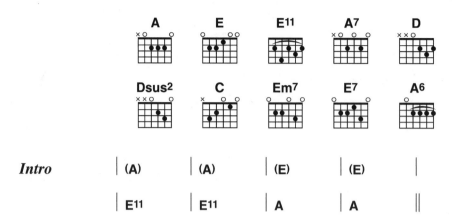

Intro | (A) | (A) | (E) | (E) |

| E11 | E11 | A | A ‖

Chorus 1

N.C.   A
C'mon take me to the Mardi Gras

                      E
Where the people sing and play,

        E11
Where the dancing is elite

And there's music in the street

             A
 Both night and day.

N.C.   A
Hurry take me to the Mardi Gras

            E
In the city of my dreams.

       E11
You can legalize your laws,

You can wear your summer clothes

          A   A7
In the New Orleans.

Verse 1

And I will lay my burden   **D** down,

Rest my head upon that   **Dsus2** shore.

And when I wear that starry   **C** crown

I won't be wanting anymore.   **Em7**   **E7**

Chorus 2

N.C.   **A**

Take your burdens to the Mardi Gras,

                    E

Let the music wash your soul.

E11

You can mingle in the street,

                           A

You can jingle to the beat of the jelly roll.

Tumba, tumba, tumba, Mardi Gras

                E

Tumba, tumba, tumba, day

    E11   **A**

Yeah. _____

Coda

| A | A | E7 | E7 | |
| E11 | E11 | A6 | A6 | ‖ |

‖: A6 | A6 | E7 | E7 |

| E11 | E11 | A6 | A6 | :‖   *Repeat to fade* |

Fifty Ways To Leave Your Lover

From *Still Crazy After All These Years* (1975)

GUITARISTS HAVE LITERALLY hundreds of classic riffs to play, but it's rare that any pop song opens with a famous drum riff. Fifty Ways to Leave Your Lover features legendary session drummer Steve Gadd playing what has become one of the most popular – and difficult – drum intros in pop history.

How to play it

If you can manage a few basic barre chords, then this is probably the easiest song in the book to play. The spacious, jazzy chords of the verse are a little unusual, but thankfully they're played at a comfortably slow tempo, giving you plenty of time to change from one chord to the next.

The chords

After four bars of drums, the verse begins, with plectrum downstrokes over the chords of Em/G, D6, Cmaj7, and then a jazzy change from B7♭9 to B7 over two beats. Although many of the chord names might be new to you, take a look at the TAB below and the fretboxes over the page. Complex-sounding chords like F♯m6, D♯dim and B7aug are actually just as easy to fret as more familiar ones like G and D.

Chorus strumming

The track shifts gear dramatically when the wistful discussions of the verse become the Country bounce of the chorus. All of those ethereal jazz chords become straight major or seventh chord shapes. Note that the recording features three guitars – Paul himself, and session players Hugh McCracken & John Tropea. On the chord sheet we've shown easy open shapes of G7 and C7, but if you know barre chord versions of these, you may find you get a more lively feel from the rhythm part, and the contrast between verse and chorus will be even more dramatic.

▼ Intro

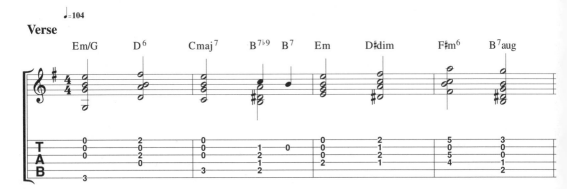

Fifty Ways To Leave Your Lover

Words & Music by Paul Simon

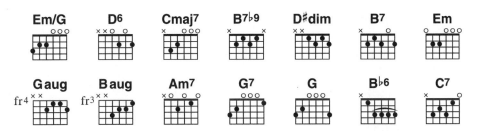

Em/G	D6	Cmaj7	B7♭9	D#dim	B7	Em

Gaug	Baug	Am7	G7	G	B♭6	C7

Intro | Drums for 4 bars ||

Verse 1

    Em/G   D6   Cmaj7   B7♭9 B7
"The problem is all inside your head", she said to me,

Em   D#dim   Gaug   Baug
"The answer is easy if you take it logically.

Em/G   D6   Cmaj7   B7♭9
I'd like to help you in your struggle to be free.

         B7   Em   Am7   Em
There must be   fifty ways to leave your lover."

Verse 2

    Em/G   D6   Cmaj7   B7♭9 B7
She said, "It's really not my habit to intrude.

        Em   D#dim   Gaug   Baug
Furthermore, I hope my meaning won't be lost or misconstrued,

          Em   D6   Cmaj7   Baug
But I'll repeat myself   at the risk of being crude:

         B7   Em   Am7   Em
There must be   fifty ways to leave your lover,

       Am7   Em
Fifty ways to leave your lover."

Chorus 1

              G7
Just slip out the back, Jack,

        B♭6
Make a new plan, Stan,

             C7
You don't need to be coy, Roy,

         G
Just get yourself free.

cont.

G7
Hop on the bus, Gus,

B♭6
You don't need to discuss much.

C7
Just drop off the key, Lee,

G
And get yourself free.

G7
Just slip out the back, Jack,

B♭6
Make a new plan, Stan,

C7
You don't need to be coy, Roy,

G
Just listen to me.

G7
Hop on the bus, Gus,

B♭6
You don't need to discuss much.

C7
Just drop off the key, Lee,

G
And get yourself free.

Verse 3

Em/G   **D6**   **Cmaj7**   **B7♭9** **B7**
   She said, "It grieves me so to see you in such pain.

         Em   **D♯dim**   **Gaug**   **Baug**
I wish there was something I could do to make you smile again."

      Em   **D6**   **Cmaj7**   **B7♭9**
I said, "I appreciate that   and would you please explain

         B7 **Em**   **Am7**   **Em**
About the fifty ways.

Verse 4

      Em/G   D6   Cmaj7   B7♭9
She said, "Why don't we both just sleep on it tonight,

    B7   Em   D♯dim   Gaug   Baug
And I believe in the morning you'll begin to see the light."

               Em   D6   Cmaj7   Baug
And then she kissed me, and I realised she probably was right:

    B7   Em   Am7   Em
There must be   fifty ways to leave your lover,

    Am7   Em
Fifty ways to leave your lover.

Chorus 2

             G7
Just slip out the back, Jack,

      B♭6
Make a new plan, Stan,

             C7
You don't need to be coy, Roy,

         G
Just get yourself free.

      G7
Hop on the bus, Gus,

         B♭6
You don't need to discuss much.

      C7
Just drop off the key, Lee,

       G
And get yourself free.

       G7
Just slip out the back, Jack,

      B♭6
Make a new plan, Stan,

           C7
You don't need to be coy, Roy,

       G
Just listen to me.

      G7
Hop on the bus, Gus,

         B♭6
You don't need to discuss much.

      C7
Just drop off the key, Lee,

       G
And get yourself free.

Coda   ‖: **Drums** :‖   _Repeat to fade_

Further Reading

If you've enjoyed this book why not check out some of the great titles below. They are available from all good music retailers and book shops, or you can visit our website: www.musicroom.com. In case of difficulty please contact Music Sales direct (see page 2).

The Chord Songbook Series

Play all your favourite hits with just a few easy chords for each song! Huge range of titles to choose from, including:

NEW! **Abba** AM959740
The Beatles NO90664
Blur AM936914
Bon Jovi AM936892
Boyzone AM956956
Bryan Adams AM963490
Eric Clapton AM956054
The Corrs AM956967
The Cranberries AM944383
The Levellers AM951445
Metallica AM944680
Alanis Morissette AM944086
Oasis AM936903
Oasis 2 AM951478
Pulp AM942678
Paul Simon PS11485
Stereophonics AM956065
Sting AM940489
Stone Roses AM951500
Paul Weller AM942546
Wet Wet Wet AM938135
The Who AM956021

Play Guitar With...Series

Play guitar and sing along with the specially-recorded CD backing tracks for classic songs from your favourite bands. Here are just some of the titles in this superb series.

The Beatles NO90665
The Beatles Book 2 NO90667
The Beatles Book 3 NO90689
Blur AM935320
Bon Jovi AM92558
Bryan Adams AM963380
Eric Clapton AM950862
Eric Clapton Book 2 AM96289
The Kinks AM951863
Kula Shaker AM943767
Metallica AM92559
Oasis AM935330
Ocean Colour Scene AM943712
Simon & Garfunkel PS11516
Paul Simon PS11469
Sting AM968000
The Stone Roses AM943701

...plus many more titles for you to collect!